COOK YOURSELF

IN PRAYER

"Come Out and Manifest!"

COOK YOURSELF

IN PRAYER

"Come Out and Manifest!"

Angela Reynolds
Charles Reynolds

Paperback ISBN 978-1-66785-389-5

Digital ISBN 979-8-88722-411-4

Visit the authors' page at www.positiveauthorsmind.com.

Dedication

This book is dedicated to our beautiful children, Prophet Jaron, Prophet Chad, and Prophetess Madison.

Appreciation

We thank the Holy Spirit for guiding us through this revelatory experience and our ministry's many brethren, friends, families, and followers.

Matthew 6:9-13, *Pray like this: Our Father in Heaven, may your name be kept holy. May your Kingdom come soon. May your will be done on Earth, as it is in Heaven. Give us today the food we need, and forgive us our sins, as we have forgiven those who sin against us. And don't let us yield to temptation, but rescue us from the evil one." (NLT)*

Introduction

Prayer has been a phenomenon for centuries, dating back to the days of the Old Testament and today in the New Testament. Many biblical characters such as Abraham, Jacob, Job, David, Elijah, and others prayed earnestly by travailing in the spirit. In the New Testament, Jesus spent much time praying in Mount Olive and the Garden of Gethsemane. Additionally, he taught His disciples to pray when they struggled in their prayer lives. Apostle Paul prayed without ceasing for the churches, especially the church at Ephesus.

Some people see *prayer* as a way to talk to God, who does not judge unjustly and allows them to release their innermost thoughts (good or bad). While many people may experience instant gratifications, there are times when our prayers seem to go unanswered. Questions such as, *"Why did God let this happen?" "How could a God who loves us allow the earthquake to kill many people after sincere prayers?" "Where was God when I needed him the most?"* The questions are ongoing, yet many believers continue to communicate with our Heavenly Father intimately in times of distress and great need.

The answers to all these questions may indeed seem far away. *Why does God allow good people to die instead of saving them?* This might come as a shocker; we assume that we are "***good***," but by whose merit or qualifications do we consider ourselves "***good***"? *Ours? Men? God's?* If we are all "***good***," we should live in a "*flawless*" world without challenges or disappointments. One in which God is not needed. Therefore, we would not need to pray in this "*perfect world.*"

We are called to live a life that pleases God, serves Him in Spirit and truth, and be prosperous, even in a tainted '*world*' with all its gruesomeness.

There are rewards for seeking God's face, communicating with Him, and giving ourselves in ***prayer***. It is essential to learn how to pray and put the "*right ingredients*" to stir a fragrance that can only happen when we "*cook in prayer.*"

Author's Notes

All references to Greek and Hebrew words are taken from the Hebrew–Greek Key Word Study Bible, New Testament Greek Lexicon, and Thayer's Greek Lexicon. The Merriam-Webster and Oxford Language Dictionaries are used for general word meanings. The scriptures are taken from different bible versions (See Bible References).

TABLE OF CONTENTS

Part 1: FOUNDATION OF PRAYER

Part 2: DIMENSIONS OF PRAYER

Part 3: PROPHETIC RELEVANCE

Part 4: LET US PRAY

Bonus:

PART I:

FOUNDATION OF PRAYER

CHAPTER ONE

What is Prayer?

> *Luke 18:1, And Jesus spoke a parable unto them to this end, that men ought to always to pray and not faint. KJV*

Prayer can be thought of as uttering or communicating words to our Heavenly Father that comes from our inner thoughts. Others have defined *prayer* as an invocation or direct communication to God.

The Merriam-Webster dictionary defines *"prayer"* as an address (such as a petition) to God or a god in word or thought." The Thesaurus defines *"prayer"* as an address to God or a deity.

In a broad sense, *prayer* is *"raising the mind to God."* It is *"spiritual communication between man and God, a two-way relationship where man should talk to God and listen to Him."*

Prayer is a spirit that allows man to engage God and His host in conversation. It is the Holy Spirit that prays with us. We gain such access through His Son, Jesus Christ. We are communicating with our Heavenly Father in an intimate conversation. Beware that as we engage God, we have stirred up the kingdom of darkness whose aim is to destroy us.

Tefillah is the Hebrew word for *prayer*. In the Hebrew Bible, *prayer* is an informal petition to God or an evolving means of interacting and conversing with God. *Prayer* is spontaneous, unorganized, and, most importantly, a way to build a relationship as an individual with God, the Father.

While over six hundred prayers are recorded in the bible, Jews mostly use two types of prayer: *Shema* and *Amidah*. The *Shema* is even more important because it focuses on one's faith and knowing that only one God exists. This principle is monotheistic. Further examination shows that this is one of the foundational principles of the Torah. *Deuteronomy 6:4, "Hear O Israel, the Lord our God, the Lord is One" (NIV)*. The *Shema* is a covenant between God and the Jewish people; they usually pray three times a day.

The *Amidah* is the second most important prayer in Judaism. It is used in worship services. *Amidah, "the standing prayer,"* consists of 19 blessings. When it is being recited, the Jews face the direction of Jerusalem. This discipline and dedication come from the place of reverence for the God of Israel.

Both prayers show how *prayer* must be seen as a time to interact with the Ancient of Days, the only true and living God.

The Need for Communication

The word *"communication"* can be defined as how individuals exchange information through a standard system of symbols, signs, or behavior. In Hebrew and Greek, the word *"communicate"* is represented by more than one word: *to talk with,* **dialaleō** *(Luke 6:11); to converse with,* **homilieo** *(Luke 22:4).* In *1 Timothy 6:18, "willing to communicate"* is a single word *koinonikoi.*

Communication is an integral part of our daily life. It is the central point of human interaction. Being able to **communicate** is a gift from God. When we speak, we are imparting something to another.

Prayer is supposed to be a two-way conversation between man and God. It is a *"spiritual"* communication within a spiritual network that directly connects to God. When you **communicate** with a friend, you entrust them with some of your innermost thoughts, hoping they will give you clarity, direction, and support. Likewise, when we come before God, we need to have a conversation that shows we depend on him. If we go before him with doubt, we cannot produce results.

Why Do We Pray?

Jesus and his disciples traveled across many regions and territories to heal, deliver, and restore the broken-hearted. As Jesus developed more in his ministry, he became aware as a leader that he must not only pray but teach his disciples the art of praying effectively. He taught them the "Our Father" prayer.

As mentioned earlier, *prayer* communicates with God the Father and the Holy Spirit. Jesus knew that *prayer* was a time for an intimate conversation with his Heavenly Father. He explained that *prayer* was not for public showing and using meaningless words. In *Matthew 6:1,* Jesus said, *"Watch out! Don't do your good deeds publicly, to be admired by others"* *(NLT)*. This does not mean that we cannot pray with others. *Prayer* is and should always be sincere and without ulterior motive. We are always praying for the will of God.

The disciples thought that they knew how to pray. The Gentiles in the synagogues were competing religiously. This violated the spiritual realm, and the prayers were ineffective. *Luke 11:1, One day, Jesus was praying in a certain place. When he finished, one of his disciples said to him, "Lord, teach us to pray, just as John taught his disciples" (KJV).* Within that moment, Jesus saw the yearning and sincerity of their hearts, and he taught them how to pray. This was the first time he prayed the "Our Father" prayer.

When Should We Pray?

There is no time that the Children of God cease praying. *Prayer* is an ongoing conversation with our Heavenly Father. In Islam, Muslims are allowed to pray anytime, but there are specific times *"designated"* for certain prayers: *Fajr* (pre-dawn), *Dhuhr* (noon), *Asr* (afternoon), *Maghrib* (sunset), and *Isha* (evening). For the Christian believer, Jesus did not give specific times to pray. We are constantly praying. Our mind prays, our heart prays, and our spirit prays. However, there are **specific hours** that the enemy comes to enact his devious plans (*See Prophetic Prayer Watches*).

King David and Daniel both prayed three times a day. *Psalms 55:16-17, David proclaimed, "As for me, I will call upon God, and the Lord shall save me. Evening and morning, and at* noon I will pray, and cry aloud, and He shall hear my voice" (NKJV). Both men understood how to access the gates in the secret place they journeyed through the realm of prayer.

Peter, the Apostle, would pray three times a day. He prayed at the third hour (9 am) – *Acts 2:15*, the sixth hour (noon or noon) – *Acts 10:9*, and the ninth hour (3 pm) – *Acts 3:1*.

While the Bible gives these examples, it is not the only time that men prayed and in no way suggests that these are the only times to pray. Jesus commanded men to always be in prayer and remain steadfast. *Luke 18.1, "Then He (Jesus) spoke a parable to them, 'that men always ought to pray and not lose heart" (NKJV).*

How Should We Pray?

There is no exact method of **how we should pray**. Many people believe they have not prayed if they are not in a horizontal position or on their knees. When Jesus prayed, he used different positions: praying on his knees, standing, sitting, and even being prone. Jesus sometimes fell prostrate (face to the ground) and prayed. *Matthew 26:39, Going a little farther, he fell with his face to the ground and prayed, "My Father, if it is possible, may this cup be taken from me. Yet not as I will, but as you will" (NIV).*

Daniel prayed three times daily on his knees (*Daniel 6:10*). David laid down praying while covered in sackcloth and ashes (*2 Samuel 12:16*). Yet, David also prayed with his hands

raised (*Psalms 141:2*). Moses and Aaron fell on their faces to plead Israel's case before God (*Numbers 16:22*).

Jesus did not give specifics on what is the correct position to pray. This decision is based on your relationship and commitment to God. Remember, there is a time and place for everything. Find that secret place where you can meet with your Heavenly Father. Whether searching within yourself, releasing your feelings, or laughing with God (Yes, God has a sense of humor), you need to find that part of you that understands that our Lord is a friend like no other.

Study Question(s): Have I been communicating with God daily? How can I reorganize my prayer life?

_____

_____

_____

_____

_____

_____

_____

_____

_____

_____

_____

_____

_____

CHAPTER TWO

The Spirit of God

> *2 Corinthians 5:17, Therefore, if anyone is in Christ, he is a **new** creation; old things have passed away; behold, all things have become new. KJV*

The Beginning of Creation

From the beginning of time, *prayer* has been active throughout the universe. The *Spirit of God* has been a communicator with God before time existed. God created the Heavens and the Earth. The Bible tells us that the *Spirit of God* moved upon the face of the waters (*Genesis 1:2*). God spoke with the Holy Spirit to communicate His plans and intimate desires for the Heavenly and Earthly realms. The Earth was unformed, covered under the oceans when the *Spirit of God* started making intercession as it communicated the will of God concerning the planet.

Prayer allows the human spirit to communicate with the *Spirit of God*. It stretches us to a place where we become one with our Father within his divine presence. *Romans 8:26, "In certain ways we are weak, but the Spirit is here to help* us. For example, when we don't know what to pray for, the Spirit prays for us in ways that cannot be put into words" (CEV). The language spoken between the spirit-man and God is enclosed within a spiritual domain, bringing the spirit-man in submission to the Father's will. This is the spirit that raised Jesus from the dead after he prayed in the Garden of Gethsemane (*Mark 14:32*) for his Father's will to be done.

Before we came to Earth, we existed somewhere. As the Earthly Realm released the sounds of creation, man's spirit awakened to echo the sentiments of the **Spirit of God**. God reflected His nature and glory on Earth when He walked into dust through us, His earthly entities (man).

Intimacy of God

Prayer is a migration process into the presence of God. It is a journey into **intimacy with God**. Lucifer desired that intimacy with God, but it was given to man. So, he rebelled.

Adam was able to find **intimacy with God**. There was a deep bond as the Father communicated with him daily. The Bible tells us that God's voice came walking into the Garden of Eden looking for Adam in the cool of the day. God would have conversations with Adam and Eve in the garden. Just imagine the threesome having a conversation. Adam's alignment with God kept the Spirit and Earthly Realms as one *(See Chapter 4)*. However, Adam failed and caused the seal to be broken. He lost the ability to stay in the garden. Both Adam and his wife, Eve, were no longer welcomed. *Why*? The Garden of Eden's rulers (Adam and Eve) were tarnished. Sin had been introduced.

As we pray and engage God in conversations, we progress into the Spirit. You cannot be in the flesh and the Spirit simultaneously. *Romans 8:9, "You are no longer ruled by your desires, but by God's Spirit, who lives in you. People who don't have the Spirit of Christ in them don't belong to him"* (CEV). Your life in the flesh must end to live in the Spirit.

The journey into **intimacy with God** is where we travel into the spirit vertically and horizontally. Horizontal travel in the Spirit is one where you are *"impactful,"* and Vertical travel in the Spirit is where you find *"intimacy"* with God. While both are important, your intimacy with God will take your prayer to a level that subdues your enemies and saves you and your loved ones.

The Composition of Man

Man is made up of a spirit, soul, and body. *Pneuma* is the Greek word for *"spirit."* Our Spirit allows us to operate in the Spirit Realm while our body is of the Earthly Realm. John speaks about the intimacy in our relationship with our Heavenly Father; *John 4:24, "God [is] a Spirit: and they who worship him must worship [him] in spirit and truth"* (KJV).

Psyche is the Greek word for "*soul*," where our mind, will, and emotions dwell. Here lie our desires and feelings. When we have specific wishes, it impacts how we pray. Our minds, will, and emotions are at work when we pray. They work hand in hand. We must understand that our soul is that part of us that brings together the body and spirit of man.

Soma is the Greek word for "*body*," our earthly vessel or the house in which our spirit resides. Our body is the pathway through which the soul operates. It's made of flesh which comprises elements (*chemicals, molecules, tissues, etc.*). The body can regenerate flesh when it is harmed.

God formed us from dust and breathed life into us. He walked into dust when he created us from his innermost self. Therefore, God is inside you. You think like him and have his nature. We do not wrestle against flesh and blood but principalities and powers. He commanded us to take dominion over the Earth. We are made from the Earth (*dust*), so we must take control of the flesh.

God only communicates with the spirit-man, not the flesh. He sent his only begotten son, Jesus Christ, to redeem us. Jesus already conquered the flesh. The flesh only works against us because we do not know who we are. It is the Spirit that makes intercession for us. Paul reminds us that God abolished the enmity in his flesh and the Law to make us become one with our Father. Through his son Jesus Christ, we can access and reconcile as one through the cross (*Ephesians 3*).

Study Question(s): How can I become more intimate with God in prayer?

_____

_____

_____

_____

_____

_____

_____

_____

_____

_____

_____

_____

_____

_____

CHAPTER THREE

Separating One's Self

> *2 Corinthians 5:17, Anyone who belongs to Christ is a new person. The past is forgotten, and everything is new. CEV*

Submission to God's Will

The *soul* comprises the mind, will, desires, and emotions. Our mind is the main target of the enemy. Satan uses the weapon of lies to contradict God's desires and will for our life. If he can control the mind, our will, emotions, and passions become affected. Man has been given a free choice. That means we have the opportunity to choose between good and evil. *Romans 12:2, "Don't copy the behavior and customs of this world but let God transform you into a new person by changing the way you think. Then you will learn to know God's will for you, which is good and pleasing and perfect"* (NLT).

The Children of God experience many blessings in today's world and face many challenges. Our intuition can become compromised based on what we experience. The mind can interact with intuition and cause emotions to impact how we think and communicate. We need total surrender and commitment through our Lord Jesus Christ to overcome. *John 15:7, "If you remain in Me and My words remain in you [that is if we are vitally united and My message lives in your heart], ask whatever you wish, and it will be done for you"* (AMP).

God's will is the blueprint he has provided for His creation. His will can be viewed as his *"choice," "decision,"* or *"plans"* for our lives. It is essential to ask God to let his will be done as it is in heaven. Yielding to God allows the Holy Spirit to have His way in your life.

The Bible tells us in *Psalms 143:10, "Teach me to do Your will, For You are my God; Let Your good Spirit lead me on level ground"* (KJV). When you walk in the Spirit, the blood of Jesus cleans the system. Apostle Paul admonished the saints in *Romans 13* to live **"not according to the flesh"** but by the Spirit.

Submission to God's will (His authority) brings us freedom. It allows the spirit-man within us to walk the path of righteousness. *Galatians 5:25, "If we live by the Spirit, let us also walk by the Spirit"* (NIV). We become separated from the things of this world because our steps are ordered. The flesh no longer has power over us. The result? We arrive at intimacy with God and experience spiritual authority (dominion). Dominion is the verdict of intimacy.

Forgiveness

Jesus explained that men always should be prayerful. Sometimes, we find that the things of the past burden us. The hurt and pain of losing a loved one, our personal belongings, being abandoned, terminated, or laid off from a job, and other life factors can cause depression. Resentment, the embarrassment of failure, and feelings of rejection are emotions that can easily take over the human body. We need to let go and allow God to mold us.

Forgiving yourself and others bring forth healing to the human soul. In *Psalms 51:1*, David cried to God, *"Have mercy upon me, O God, according to thy lovingkindness: according unto the multitude of thy tender mercies, blot out my transgressions"* *(KJV)*. King David recognized that he had limitations. He had sent Uriah into battle, committed adultery with Uriah's wife, Bathsheba, and gotten her pregnant. He knew that many people had their perceptions of his actions. With all that David had done, he became overwhelmed by guilt about his failing God. However, he had unwavering faith in

God. He learned to forgive himself and others. He asked God to forgive him of his trespasses.

Submission to God's will means letting go of pain and hurt against those who have despitefully used you. God requires us to walk righteously and be at peace with others as much as possible. Most importantly, forgive yourself.

Forgiveness in *prayer* is necessary for the individual to have full access to God. Jesus forgave the thief on the cross as he cried to his Heavenly Father. *Prayer* helps us release those burdens from feelings of guilt and hurts of the past. We must let go and allow God to fill our hearts' void.

Our Heart Prays Too

The *heart* is a muscular organ about the size of a fist, located just behind and slightly left of the breastbone. It is the primary organ of our circulatory system. The *heart* is constantly communicating with the brain. Our emotions change the signals it sends to the brain. It significantly impacts our *hearts* when we feel sad, happy, or pressured.

As we enter into *prayer*, the brain communicates with the *heart* our intentions. The *heart* responds, and our body experiences the emotions we feel as we pray. At times, we see people becoming very emotional, experiencing a loss of words because they cannot explain the joy or sadness they are feeling. They go through the ***Realm of Prayer*** as they spiritually journey into God.

Prayer connects us to the *heart* of God. Sometimes, we feel empty, and no words come from our mouths. We don't need to utter words as the spirit-man in us communicates with God, the Father. Therefore, our *heart* prays too.

Study Question(s): Have I completely surrendered myself to God? Is my will more important than God's Will?

_____

_____

_____

_____

_____

_____

_____

_____

_____

_____

_____

_____

_____

_____

PART II:

DIMENSIONS OF PRAYER

CHAPTER FOUR

Entering the Spiritual Realm

> *Colossians 3:1-3, You have been raised to life with Christ. Now set your heart on what is in heaven, where Christ rules at God's right side. Think about what is up there, not about what is here on earth. You died, which means that your life is hidden with Christ, who sits beside God. CEV*

The Realm

The separation of powers due to the war in Heaven has created catastrophic scenarios and challenges for those who have received the Lord Jesus Christ as their Savior. *Psalm 34:19, "Many are the afflictions of the righteous, But the LORD delivers him out of them all" (KJV).*

Different **realms** operate according to their purpose within the universe. Before the creation of time, God existed in a place without time. He created time for His will to take place. When Adam broke the laws in the Spirit, time was introduced to give humanity a second opportunity at reconciliation with God, our creator.

The more prevalent realms are the **Heavenly Realm,** the **Demonic Realm,** and **the Earthly or Human Realm.** Within the Heavenly and Demonic Realm is the **Spirit Realm.** The Spirit Realm is the balance between all the realms.

Each realm operates according to the authority it is given. Many Apostles and Prophets often say, **"I see in the Realm of the Spirit,"** or **"In the Realm of the Spirit."** They have been given access to a realm where God reveals secrets and revelations for his people (individuals, family, etc.), the church, world events, the governments, and the nations.

The order of operation in the realms is based on the hierarchy of the leadership, which is highly organized and influential in the roles given. God is Alpha, Omega, Beginning, and the End; He is before time begins and will reign after time ends.

The Heavenly Realm

Within the **Heavenly Realm** is the Lord's Host/Lord's Army, the Council, the Archangels, Spirit Beings, Jesus Christ, and the Holy Spirit (able to come and go). Each division comprises a leadership body that includes Princes and Captains/Commanders. *Joshua 5: 13-14, "Now when Joshua was near Jericho, he looked up and saw a man standing in* *front of him with a drawn sword in His hand. Joshua approached Him and asked, "Are You for us or our enemies?" "Neither," He replied. "I have now come as commander of the LORD's army." Then Joshua fell facedown in reverence and asked Him, "What does my Lord have to say to His servant?" (NIV)*

There have been numerous debates about whether God lives in Heaven. *Isaiah 66:1, The LORD says: "Heaven is my throne, and the Earth is my footstool. Where is the house you will build for me? Where will my resting place be?" (NIV).* It would be fitting to say, "God's dwelling place is in our hearts." In the Book of Enoch, Chapter 22, Enoch's vision shows him being transported to the tenth heaven. There he saw the face of the Lord. In the second book of *Enoch 22:1, "In the 10th Heaven, the archangel Michael brought Enoch in front of the face of the LORD."*

God positioned the Heavenly Realm as one where authority has been given. If Heaven is God's throne, we must understand that it is where laws in the Spirit are established. Therefore, we have kingdom authority! *Why?* It is our inheritance! Those that accept Christ are Christ-purchased because the Holy Spirit has sealed us (*Ephesians 1*).

The Word of God reminds us that *Matthew 18:18, "Truly I tell you, whatever you bind on Earth will be bound in Heaven, and whatever you loose on Earth will be loosed in Heaven"* (NIV). The **Heavenly Realm** reacts on our behalf when we use our God-given authority. We must let the enemy know that we speak from a higher kingdom; the Kingdom of God. We are backed by the Lord's host when we walk in God's will and understand that our access to God is through his Son, Jesus Christ.

Demonic Realm

The **Kingdom of Darkness** can be likened to an organized criminal structure in which roles are given depending on the level of evil intent. There are kings, queens, emperors, empresses, princes, princesses, and other titles. The **Demonic Realm** reflects a hierarchy in which the leader, Lucifer, who operates in his office as Satan, also known as the Devil, is assisted by his fellow fallen angels, demons, and evil spirits. Some Bible scholars believe that Satan was inducted as the Captain of the Underworld/Hades and inherently initiated as the Prince of Persia.

The **Demonic Realm** is subdivided as follows: the Kingdom of Darkness (the residence of Lucifer, King of Persia), the

Fallen Angels Realm, and the Operating forces of the Underworld. Within each subdivision are jurisdictions that cannot be crossed. Everyone must operate within their domain and the level of rank. At times, the Demonic Realm experiences chaos, as demons and fallen angels fight against each other to gain territorial access and favor from their leader (Satan). They will even kill each other. Additionally, disagreements with those in authority are evident.

During Daniel's twenty-one days of prayer and fasting, the Prince of Persia intercepted and tried to stop the answers to Daniel's prayers (received from the Heavenly throne) from reaching him. The archangel Gabriel became detained by the Prince of Persia until the archangel, Michael, Prince of God, came and rescued him from the Prince of Persia. *Daniel 10:12-13, "Do not be afraid, Daniel," he said, "for from the first day that you purposed to understand and humble yourself before your God, your words were heard, and I have come in response to them. But the prince of the Persian kingdom resisted me for twenty-one days. Then Michael, one of the chief princes, came to help me because I was detained there with the king of Persia" (NKJV).*

While many disagree that the Prince of Persia is Satan, a fallen angel or territorial spirit, it is commonly agreed that

Satan overthrew the domain of dark powers after being eliminated from the Heavens. This resulted in his claim to the throne within the **Demonic Realm** as the Prince of the Dark Underworld and becoming the ruler of darkness.

The Demonic Realm's primary purpose is to control the

Heavenly and Human Realms. Demons and fallen angels must secure their positions and worthiness within their realm. They can demonize the sinner or oppress the believer through fear and oppression, deception, and depression. As you pray, you may encounter weariness, falling asleep, loss of words to speak, feelings of heaviness, and even anger. Remember, Satan has three main goals: *to steal, kill, and destroy (John 10:10, KJV).* It is imperative to keep praying and PUSH (Pray Until Something Happens). While your strength may fail, God's strength is perfect for your weakness.

Earthly or Human Realm

The **Earthly Realm** represents God's desire to have a relationship with someone other than himself. God and His Council discussed creating another embodiment of himself that would rule the Earth. God created man to rule over every living thing and Earth's structures. The idea was that humanity would reflect God's Earthly nature as the

Heavenly Realm showed his Spirit nature in action.

Earth has three layers: the crust, the mantle, and the core. Seventy percent of the Earth is water and thirty percent land. Like Earth, God created man with a body, spirit, and soul. The body (*crust*) is the Earthly vessel that is our makeup or physical features as human beings. This part reflects our experiences (happiness, sadness, pain, and hurt), physical injuries from a broken bone to a cut. The spirit (*mantle*) is that part of man that cannot be seen but is the connecting force where the unknown language is uttered between man and God. It is where the soul rests. The soul (*core*) is that gateway through the body and spirit. It is the core of our existence where the natural man experiences desires and emotions based on his free will. Without the soul, man cannot exist.

God's desires are different from those of Satan. Satan has never seen God because God is the "Father of Lights." *1 Timothy 6:16, "He alone is immortal and dwells in unapproachable light. No one has ever seen Him, nor can anyone see Him. To Him be honor and eternal dominion! Amen"* (BSB). He created man to be like a God within the Earthly Realm, and Satan has a problem with that. *Why?* He was not given that authority.

In *Genesis 3:14*, God told the serpent that he would crawl on his belly and eat dust for the rest of his life. What is dust? Man is dust because he was created from dust. Therefore, Satan will continue to torment humans until man realizes the depth of his authority in God. Man will experience the natural disasters, the excruciating pains of hardship, the fleshly desires, and the challenges of human nature. It is the consequences that we must face because Adam broke the laws of God and human nature. The covenant between man and God was broken. Therefore, the Demonic Realm will continue to work against us by wreaking havoc on the Earthly Realm, securing its position as the dominating force, and removing the dominion given to man.

Remember, God sent his only begotten Son, Jesus Christ, to redeem us from the sins of Adam and reconcile with him, our Heavenly Father. He affirmed man's role and jurisdiction of the government and those in authority within the Earthly Realm. *Luke 19:10, Jesus said, "the Son of Man has come to seek and save the lost" (KJV).*

The Spiritual Realm

It is within the *Spiritual Realm* that spiritual warfare takes place. The kingdom of darkness consistently tries to gain the upper hand within this realm. Adam's alignment with God preserved the **Spiritual Realm**. His failure brought *iniquity* upon humanity. Jesus came to Earth; he established the rule and power over all realms. *John 14:6, Jesus answered, "I am the way, truth, and life. No one comes to the Father except through Me" (BSB)*. Therefore, he had the authority to take control of Heaven and Earth. *Matthew 6:9, "Thy kingdom come. Thy will be done on Earth as it is in Heaven" (KJV)*.

Many Christians do not understand that they must be in **prayer** to enter the **Spiritual Realm**. The *"gates"* of the **Spiritual Realm prayer**. Within this realm, even our thoughts can speak. The Bible tells us in *Ephesians 6, "For our struggle is not against flesh and blood, but against the rulers, against the authorities, against the powers of this dark world, and against the spiritual forces of evil in the Heavenly Realms" (NIV)*. These are activities that take place within the spiritual realm every second.

It is essential to understand that **"righteous"** is the power of the Kingdom of God, and **"sin"** is the power of the kingdom of darkness. There are continued conflicts between God's Angels and the satanic forces. Such battles are fought within the **Spiritual Realm** on behalf of their domains. **Prayer** is the portal we must use to access God's throne at all times.

The Realms of Prayer and Worship

The *Spiritual Realm* consists of different "domains" that oversee the plan of God for our lives. These are subsidiaries within God's spiritual network. Many Spirit beings carry out God's requests and mandates daily. In *1 Kings 22:22*, Prophet Micaiah prophesied against King Ahab, who had gone against God's will. *"Then a spirit came forward, stood before the LORD, and said, 'I will entice him.' 'By what means?' asked the LORD. And he replied, 'I will go out and be a lying spirit in the mouths of all his prophets.' 'You will surely entice him and prevail,' said the LORD. 'Go and do it"* (BSB).

The Spirit of Prayer and the Spirit of Worship are charged with bringing us into the *Realms of Prayer and Worship*. We cannot enter these realms without getting access through the gates. Worship brings us to a place where the voice of God is released in us as we make room for the Holy Spirit. We are quickened and stirred up through the Holy Spirit to enter the Gates of Prayer. Knowing how to worship and pray in Spirit gives us access to the *Realms of Prayer and Worship*.

The Gates of Prayer takes us within an atmosphere where our thoughts can speak on our behalf as the Spirit of God makes intercession. We must know how to ignite the fire within us and be eager to commune with God. He wants to restore His voice to His people and fulfill His purpose in our lives.

One of the things Satan uses against us is our inability to see in the spirit. He is a master masquerader and disguises himself in many ways to inflict pain upon God's people. So many people have lost their *"praise"* because of the pressures of life. We need to be able to go deeper in prophetic prayer and worship and travel in the Spirit to see and hear God's voice.

Study Question(s): What realms do you consider the most important? What do they have in common? How are they different?

_____

_____

_____

_____

_____

_____

_____

_____

_____

_____

_____

_____

_____

_____

CHAPTER FIVE

The Courts of Heaven

> *Revelations 4:2, At once I was in [special communication with] the Spirit; and behold, a throne stood in heaven, with One seated on the throne. AMP*

What are the Courts of Heaven?

The word *"court"* has several meanings in the English Language. According to the Merriam-Webster dictionary, the term *"court"* refers to 1. the residence or establishment of a sovereign or similar dignitary; 2. a place (such as a chamber) for the administration of justice; 3. a manor house or large building surrounded by usually enclosed grounds. For this book, we will focus on the second meaning.

The term *courts* referred to the temple or part of the temple where God was enthroned in the Old Testament. In the New Testament, the *courts* were a legal place of business to bring charges against someone.

Many believers think they are free from attack because they have Jesus Christ as their savior. We must be aware that we are being accused by the enemy daily. Satan stands before daily, accusing the saints and reminding them of their sins. As in the Earthly Realm, there are consequences when man violates the law; Likewise, we are given spiritual tickets and fines for violations in the Spirit. These are some things that Satan uses against us in the *Courts of Heaven*.

The *Court of Heaven* or *Courts of Heaven* is where justice is carried out. It is where Satan, the accuser, announces his accusations against the Children of God. In the *Court of Heaven*, Jesus is our mediator and advocate. The Court is where God pours out His wrath against the enemy and releases judgments based on the evidence and arguments presented.

Types of Court

Psalms 82:1, God presides in the great assembly; he renders judgment among the "gods" (NIV).

1. The Court of Mediation

2 Corinthians 5:18, "Now all things are of God, who has reconciled us to Himself through Jesus Christ, and has given us the ministry of reconciliation" (NKJV). This court is where Jesus Christ mediates between the accuser and us. Only him, Jesus Christ, can reconcile us to God the Father.

2. The **Court of Petition**

Philippians 4:6, "Do not be anxious about anything, but in every situation, by prayer and petition, with thanksgiving, present your requests to God" (NIV). You **must** request an audience and deliver your petition(s) before God.

3. **The Throne of Grace**

Hebrews 4:16, "Let us then approach God's throne of grace with confidence so that we may receive mercy and find grace to help us in our time of need" (NIV). We must confess our sins and ask God for grace and mercy.

4. **The Court of Mount Zion**

Hebrews 12:22–24, "But you have come to Mount Zion, to the city of the living God, the Heavenly Jerusalem. You have come to thousands upon thousands of angels in joyful assembly, to the church of the firstborn, whose names are written in Heaven. You have come to God, the Judge of all, to the spirits of the righteous made perfect, to Jesus the mediator of a new covenant, and to the sprinkled blood that speaks a better word than the blood of Abel" *(NIV)*. The blood of Jesus speaks for us, so stand on the word and remind God of his promises. The Throne of Grace works together with this court.

5. **The Court of the Accuser**

Revelation 12:10, "For the accuser of our brothers and sisters, who accuses them before our God day and night, has been hurled down" (NIV). Satan presents his evidence against us. Within this court, Jesus Christ is our advocate.

6. **Court of the Ancient of Days (Supreme Court)**

Daniel 7:9–10, "As I looked, "thrones were set in place, the Ancient of Days took his seat. His clothing was as white as snow; The hair of his head was white like wool. His throne was flaming with fire, and its wheels were all ablaze. A river of fire was flowing, coming out from before him. Thousands upon thousands attended him; ten thousand times, ten thousand stood before him. The court was seated, and the books were opened" (NIV). In this court, God has the final say. Pray for a favorable verdict.

The Armor of God

Ephesians 6:10-18 reminds us to put on the Armor of God because we do not wrestle against flesh and blood but principalities and powers in high places. The weapon of spiritual warfare is prayer. However, we cannot enter battle without having armor.

In the Earthly Army, countries gather against the enemies to defend their territories, take something by force, or show their power stance. Every soldier put on protective gear in uniforms, armors, etc. Note that the positions in terms of ranks determine the dress code for each soldier. Within the Spiritual Realms, God's host understands the meaning of warfare. It is a spiritual battle that can manifest into an Earthly struggle within the Human Realm.

When praying in spiritual warfare, the Child of God must put on the Armor of God. *Ephesians 6:11-12, "Put on all the armor that God gives so that you can defend yourself against the devil's tricks. We are not fighting against humans. We are fighting against forces and authorities and against rulers of darkness and powers in the spiritual world." (CEV).*

There are seven pieces of armor that God requires man to put on to be **ready** at all times. We must understand that spiritual warfare is not something we must expose ourselves to without having the proper gear; we will be harmed. We need our spiritual clothes just as much as our physical clothes.

1. *"Gird your loins with truth"* (*Ephesians 6:14*). The belt of truth keeps the word of God in place. Having a secure belt means walking by faith and knowing

that what God says in His word will keep us from falling.

2. *"The Breastplate of Righteousness"* (*Ephesians 6:14*). Why the *Breastplate of Righteous*? The heart is vulnerable and a very delicate organ in our body. When we pray, our heart prays too. Sometimes, the attacks can cause the heart to become weak. We need to keep the breastplate on at all times.

3. Put on the proper footwear. We must *"shod our feet with the gospel of peace"* (*Ephesians 6:15*). Shod means wearing shoes. In life, we set goals and have decisions to make. Our feet take us into places. We must always be prepared (ready) and walk in the spirit.

4. The *"Shield of Faith"* (*Ephesians 6:16*) is the fourth armor. It is a protective barrier to withstand the devil's fiery darts. Protecting our hearts from resentment, jealousy, and unforgiveness is vital to our spiritual health. The shield can quench the fiery darts aimed at our hearts.

5. The *"Helmet of Salvation"* (*Ephesians 6:16*) protects the mind: our thoughts, desires, and emotions (soul). When Satan launches his attacks, he goes after your

mind. Having your head spiritually covered is essential to prevail against the evil one.

6. The *"Sword of the Spirit"* is the Word of God (*Ephesians 6:17*). It is a weapon of warfare and a weapon of faith. Jesus was the Living Word. He manifested practical examples that the Child of God should use daily. The Word of God is like a *"two-edged"* sword. It can heal, deliver, and set us free. However, the same expression of God becomes a weapon to destroy the enemy and his plans.

7. *"Prayer"* (*Ephesians 6:18*) is the most dangerous weapon against the enemy. *Prayer* brings us to a place of total reliance on God. The whole armor is what God gives us to face the devil's wiles. God's strength is made perfect in our weakness.

How Do We Prepare for Battle?

Before we can get a verdict, there are steps to preparing for battle. Remember, we **are not** fighting the fight. The battle belongs to the Lord. However, we **must** be ready for the attacks of the enemies. We must:

1. Understand that the forces against us are spiritual

2. beings who operate in the Demonic Realm within the kingdom of darkness.

3. There are violations in the Spirit held against us.

4. The demons operating within their realm have authority.

5. Our focus in battle is to understand that the Lord and His host are fighting on your behalf.

Operating in the Heavenly Court

In 1 Samuel 17, David knew Israel was in trouble because the Philistines terrorized the Israelites. His brothers were old enough to be soldiers, but David had to look after the sheep in his father's household. David went to give his brothers some food when he noticed how troubled the Israelites were. After inquiring about the matter and gathering information (*evidence*), David realized that the war was not only physical but spiritual.

David offered to fight Goliath because he knew God had already given us authority. Additionally, his continued time spent in ***prayer*** had given him the spiritual power to stand firm in adversity. When he realized Israel's fate was on the line, David entered the Courts of Heaven to secure a verdict against Goliath in the spiritual realm. Saul gave him physical armor, but David knew this was spiritual warfare. At this time, David's spirit-man stood in the courts on behalf of Israel. He did not see **Goliath**, the giant! He saw an "*ant*" in the spirit looking at him.

A verdict was rendered in Israel's favor and came with God's backing. *1 Samuel 17:45-46, David said to the Philistine, "You come against me with sword and spear and javelin, but I come against you in the name of the LORD Almighty, the God of the armies of Israel, whom you have defied. The Lord will deliver you into my hands this day, and I will strike you down and cut off your head. This very day I will give the carcasses of the Philistine army to the birds and the wild animals, and the whole world will know that there is a God in Israel" (NIV).*

Steps to Securing a Verdict

On Earth, there are court systems consisting of judges, plaintiffs, defendants, lawyers, and witnesses. We must understand that our battles take place in the Spiritual Realm. In the Heavenly Court, there is Satan (*accuser*), Jesus Christ (*our advocate*), the presentation of our case(s), and the verdict. To pursue, we must first secure a judgment, a decision, or a verdict. There are some steps to follow that will take us into the Courts of Heaven.

1. Take the battle into the Court of Heaven

Rev. 19:11, "Now I saw heaven opened, a white horse. And He who sat on him was called Faithful and True, and in righteousness, He judges and makes war" (BSB). We do not fight on the battlefield. The art of war is to be ahead of the enemy, so we take the battle to the courtroom.

2. **Prayer takes us into the Courtroom**

Prayer is the gate to the spiritual realm. We must pray and request an audience with the Lord. Jesus Christ has already purchased us with his blood. We should not let fear control us. Instead, we should pray and rest assured that our advocate (*1 John 2:1*) will stand before us to face the accuser.

3. **We must pray the Will of God**

1 John 5:14-15, "My purpose in writing is simply this: that you who believe in God's Son will know beyond the shadow of a doubt that you have eternal life, the reality and not the illusion. And how bold and free we become in his presence, freely asking according to his will, sure that he's listening. And if we're confident that he's listening, we know that what we've asked for is as good as ours" (MSG). We must understand that prayer has a higher purpose. When in the courtroom, remember that the accuser has come with evidence to destroy us physically, psychologically, emotionally, and physically. We must ask God for forgiveness and His will to be done on

Earth as written in Heaven.

4. Securing a Verdict

Luke 18:3-5, Jesus told them a story showing that it was necessary

for them to pray consistently and never quit. He said, "There was
once a judge in some city who never gave God a thought and cared
nothing for people. A widow in that city kept after him: 'My
rights are being violated. Protect me!' "He never gave her the time
of day. But after this went on and on, he said to himself, 'I care
nothing what God thinks, even fewer what people think. But
because this widow won't quit badgering me, I'd better do
something and see that she gets justice — otherwise, I'm going to
end up beaten black-and-blue by her pounding" (MSG).

The parable that Jesus spoke was to show if the unjust judge
could give justice. How much more will he do for you, the
believer? When we present a petition before, we ask Him
for a verdict in our favor. Be persistent with your prayers so
that God will see the earnest desires of your heart.

Study Question(s): How can I know if I am in the Courts of Heaven? Do I have any cases against me that require a verdict?

_____

_____

_____

_____

_____

_____

_____

_____

_____

_____

_____

_____

_____

_____

CHAPTER SIX

Praying in Tongues

Acts 2:3-4, They saw tongues like flames of fire that separated and came to rest on each of them. And they were all filled with the Holy Spirit and began to speak in other tongues as the

Speaking in Tongues

The term or phrase *"speaking in tongues"* is described as a form of glossolalia in which a person experiencing religious ecstasy utters incomprehensible sounds to be of divine inspiration. To put it simply, *speaking in tongues* is the utterance of unknown languages that can only be understood between God and man. Paul (Apostle) considered *speaking in tongues* the "Language of Angels."

Speaking in tongues is sometimes called "the gift of tongues." It is **one** evidence of being *"filled"* with the Holy Spirit. However, this has been highly debated between bible scholars, preachers, teachers, and many pastors.

Tongues were first heard when the disciples had gathered

to wait for the arrival of the Holy Spirit. *Acts 2:1-4, "On the day of Pentecost, all the believers were meeting together. Suddenly, there was a sound from Heaven like the roaring of a mighty windstorm filling the house where they were sitting. Then, what looked like flames or tongues of fire appeared and settled on them. And everyone present was filled with the Holy Spirit and began speaking in other languages, as the Holy Spirit gave them this ability"* (NLT).

Many scientists are mystified and have continued to study this phenomenon. They are amazed at how the brain works when someone is ***speaking in tongues***. Notably, the parts of the brain that are active while speaking in ***"Angelic language."***

Dr. Newberg, formerly a professor at the University of Pennsylvania, studied the relationship between faith and science while he was there. What he discovered was shocking and very insightful. Dr. Newberg found that the language being uttered was not any ordinary language. Additionally, the language uttered during ***"speaking in tongues"*** was not the everyday language that could activate the front lobe (of the brain). He noticed that when the participants prayed in their language, their brain activity in the frontal lobe was regular. However, when ***praying in*** *tongues*, the brain activity in the front lobe became quiet. Why? The participants explained that the Holy Spirit spoke and manifested through them. The Bible tells us in *1 Corinthians 2:12, "What we have received is not the spirit of the world, but the Spirit who is from God, so that we may understand what God has freely given us"* (NIV).

While many scientists and linguists are still puzzled at this phenomenon, the believer who has accepted Christ finds that speaking in an unknown language is special between man and God. The disciples' experiences on the Day of Pentecost were one of receiving Jesus Christ's promise that the Comforter (*the Holy Spirit*) would be with them after he was gone. As the Holy Spirit came upon them, they began *speaking in tongues* (*different languages*) never heard before.

Praying in Tongues

As mentioned previously, *praying in tongues* is dependent on the Spirit of God inhabiting the individual. The disciples were all on one accord as the Spirit of God gave them utterance. The power of God was evident, and lives were transformed that day.

Prayer is a migration process into the Spiritual Realm. It is a gateway into the supernatural. *Tongues* are direct communication with God. In *1 Corinthians 14:2*, *"For he who speaks in a tongue does not speak to men but God, for no one understands him; however, in the spirit, he says mysteries"* (BSB).

It is the Holy Spirit that inspires us as we pray in tongues. Apostle Paul explained that *tongues* edify the one who speaks it. While you may not understand what you are saying, you can find comfort in knowing that you are praying the will of God as you speak in tongues.

As you are *praying in tongues*, your Spirit is praying. Therefore, your faith becomes more vital as you pray in the heart. The more you pray in tongues, you are maximizing the gifts that God has placed in you. It helps you discover how the Holy Spirit dwells in you.

Speaking in tongues through *prayer* helps you move from the desires of the flesh to allow the will of God to be done in your life. The Holy Spirit will enable you to pray for the unknown and discover secrets only God can reveal. These divine revelations help us tap into mysteries our natural man cannot understand.

Sometimes we do not know what to pray for because they are mysteries to God. These mysteries are essential because God understands what you desire. Therefore, the Holy Spirit prays for us, manifested through tongues.

As you go deeper in **prayer**, ask God to activate the "gift of tongues" within you. It will help you pray for things beyond the scope of the human mind, such as sickness, generational curses, defeating the strongman, and securing verdicts against the kingdom of darkness.

If you are still searching, stop right now. The Holy Spirit is not lost. It is a gift already given to man. You can experience the "*supernatural*" too. Open yourself to Lord Jesus Christ and receive the Holy Spirit.

Study Question(s): What does the Word of God tell you about speaking in tongues? Have you ever spoken or prayed in tongues? If so, when was the first time you spoke in tongues?

_____

_____

_____

_____

_____

_____

_____

_____

_____

_____

_____

_____

_____

_____

PART III:
PROPHETIC RELEVANCE

CHAPTER SEVEN

A Higher Purpose to Prayer

> *Matthew 6:5, And when you pray, do not be like the hypocrites, for they love to pray standing in the synagogues and on the street corners to be seen by others. NIV*

Why Our Prayers Are Not Answered

Often, we say, "*Man of God, I've prayed, I've fasted, but nothing happened.*" We are praying amidst. *James 4:3, "When you ask, you do not receive that you may spend what you get on your pleasures because you ask with wrong motives" (NIV)*. For example, you pray and fast for forty days, and nothing happens. You pray for a house, car, a new job, and other things, but it seems as if God did not hear. Were you praying for God's will to be done or only for your fleshly desires?

Let us examine Daniel's prayer. Daniel was praying for knowledge and understanding because he wanted to walk in the will of God. His mindset was to complete his Father's will, so he prayed three times a day, confessing the sins of

Israel and petitioning God on their behalf. However, it came to a point where Daniel wanted to gain more knowledge, and he went into three weeks of prayer and fasting. His answer did not come speedily because the archangel, Gabriel, struggled to return with the answer. It was as if there were obstacles in every path. God had heard and answered the prayer because Daniel's mindset was in the right place. He prayed out of nothing until something happened. The answer was delayed until God sent an archangel with a higher rank, Michael (*Prince of God*), to see what was happening. Daniel's response was eventually delivered.

We often pray, and it seems God is not fast enough for us. We ask God for things, and the answer seems never to come. It is essential to understand that God does not come in man's time but in his own time. When our prayers seem unanswered, it doesn't mean it has been denied. It may have been delayed.

Delay is not final; it is preparation for God to do the impossible. We will experience delays at times. We experience traffic delays on streets and highways in our natural world, which can become frustrating. However, we can choose to give up or remain determined to get to our destination. Remember, Daniel's answer took three weeks because of the delays in the Spirit too. Keep holding on to the fact that God cannot fail, so we cannot fail. We cannot control how long it takes to receive the answer. However, we can control our journey to seeking God.

God's Wish for Us

God desires everyone to have everything we need according to his riches in glory. *Matthew 6:25, "That is why I tell you not to worry about everyday life — whether you have enough food and drink, or enough clothes to wear. Isn't life more than food, and your body more than clothing?"* (NLT)

As human beings, we have been given free will. God has provided us with the ability and resources to have a prosperous life. Sometimes the challenges cause many people to try to *"fix"* the situation in their way. The bills are piling up; the children are hungry; the rent or mortgage is due; the bank calls about the loan, and the list goes on and on. Yet, we find ourselves not trusting God's promises. God has promised us that he will take care of our needs.

There was a time when we both stopped working due to circumstances beyond our control. Yes, we have experienced job loss too. During that time, the mortgage was not paid and went into arrears. We invested in different businesses, and they failed. We got frustrated and angry, and our marriage came under stressful times. Yet, we still prayed in all the ways you could think of – loud, soft, aggressive, long, and short prayers. It didn't matter; it became overwhelming. We kept on asking and asking. We paid thousands of dollars to get a loan modification. Even other Prophets prayed for us (*the Prophet is subject to the Prophet*). We had to choose. When God told us to focus on building his kingdom, we obeyed and stopped running from doing His will.

During a thirty-day fast, we prayed and reminded God that he had given us the house and the jobs, but now our focus would be doing His will. We would become his voice to the nations. We went deeper into **prayer** and journeyed in the spirit. Not only was our mouth praying, but our hearts prayed earnestly too. Like God remembered Noah, Abraham, Sarah, Elizabeth, and many others, he remembered us. Our prayers may have seemed to be delayed, but in the realm of the spirit, we learned how to journey into the **Realm of Prayer**.

Fasting and Prayer

The word *"fasting"* comes from the Greek word *nesteia,* which means abstinence. Fasting in Hebrew, *ta'anit or ta'anis* in Judaism, is a fast in which one abstains from all

food and drink, including water.

Jesus Christ and his disciples observed fasts such as the Day of Atonement (Acts 27:19) which in Greek, *nestuo,* means "to abstain from food." He did not require the disciples to fast frequently. However, he admonished them in a parable, *Matthew 9:15, And Jesus replied to them, "Can the wedding guests mourn while the bridegroom is still with them? The days will come when the bridegroom is taken away from them, and then they will fast"* (AMP).

Fasting helps to restore the body to its natural state. Medical experts suggest that fasting 6 – 12 hours daily, 1 to 2 times per week, helps the body to burn fat and calories. However, spiritually, it builds the spirit-man in us. Additionally, it is an entrance into the spirit realm as the flesh must die to let the spirit-man become stronger.

There are different types of fasting, such as *"Intermittent Fasting,"* which is to fast at a specific time or follow time protocols. *"Clean Fasting"* is where none or very little food is consumed, and only water and non-caloric beverages are allowed. *"Dirty Fasting"* is the term used to describe the consumption of some calories during a fasting window.

Fasting and prayer are an integral part of a Christian's life. The believer sometimes becomes confused about when to fast or whether to fast. It depends on the individual's relationship with God. There are people that God requires specific periods of fasting and prayer. In the Old Testament, *Deuteronomy 9:9* depicts Moses' first forty-day fasting, which was a preparation period to receive the laws from God. At other times, the Israelites would fast as an expression of mourning for a king or a spouse (*1 Samuel 31:13*). Sorrow removed their appetite to eat.

In *Luke 2:36-37, "There was also a prophet named Hannah Bat-P'nu'el, of the tribe of Asher. She was a very old woman — she had lived with her husband seven years after her marriage* [37] *and had remained a widow ever since; now, she was eighty-four. She never left the Temple grounds but worshipped there night and day, fasting and praying"* (*CJB*). God had a particular assignment for Anna. As she spent time *fasting and praying,* Anna understood what it meant for the flesh to die and for the Spirit to take control of the body. She learned to journey in the Spirit and into the realm of prayer.

Fasting to the Christian or believer can be considered *"starving the flesh so that you can fill the spirit."* As you are hungry for the spirit, you are draining the voice and power of the flesh. Consider doing the fasting that best suits you. For example, someone may be able to fast for 3 – 6 hours during the day, while someone may choose to fast from evening to dawn. Do not watch religion or what men say. Instead, let the Holy Spirit direct you accordingly.

Tithing in Prayer

Tithing in prayer? Yes, you heard right! We need to understand that *prayer* keeps us from failing and holding on steadfastly. From when you wake up to when you go to sleep, you should be a place of prayer. Most importantly, the heart should always pray (*See Chapter 2*).

There are 24 hours, 1440 minutes, or 86,400 seconds a day. So, our daily prayer times should not be less than two hours and forty minutes.

Genesis 14 tells us about a man named Abram (renamed Abraham after his encounter with Melchizedek) who was a tither. He tithed not only by giving a tenth of his possessions but also by building altars wherever he went.

These altars were essential places where he would meet God in *prayer*.

In *Genesis 18*, Abraham's nephew, Lot, was in Sodom and Gomorrah when God sent His angels to issue a warning of its impending destruction. Abraham depended upon his relationship with God as he prayed for the deliverance of his relatives. He knew that he had given both physically and spiritually of himself, and he needed God's intervention on behalf of his family. He made his petition before God.

Genesis 18:23-25, Abraham stepped forward and said, "Will You really sweep away the righteous with the wicked? What if there are fifty righteous ones in the city? Will You really sweep it away and not spare the place for the sake of the fifty righteous ones who are there? Far be it from You to do such a thing – to kill the righteous with the wicked so that the righteous and the wicked are treated alike. Far be it from You! Will not the Judge of all the earth do what is right?" (BSB). God answered Abraham, who had spent time journeying and *"tithing into prayer."* Abraham held God accountable for his promises that he would be the possessor of the Earth.

Our daily lives consist of many routines: taking care of the house, a spouse, children, getting to work or school, completing work or class assignments, and others based on our needs. Many people ask, *"How can I find time to pray?"* *"Do you know what I am going through?"* Sometimes, we may experience exhaustion, feel overwhelmed, or avoid prayer altogether. We must remember that God is the one that allows us to complete all these tasks.

Yes, our time is limited by the many situations we face daily. However, God's time belongs to Him and Him only. The word of God tells us that God is jealous, and He will not give his glory to others. *Isaiah 42:8, "I am the LORD; that is my name; my glory I give to no other, nor my praise to carved idols" (KJV).* We should not let our daily routine become an idol in our lives. The bible tells us to give unto Caesar what is his and unto God what belongs to him.

Praying for two hours and forty minutes does not have to be continuous. We must always be praying even as we are working. There should be continued conversations between our Heavenly Father and us. *Why?* When we need him, we expect him to show up. Are we showing up when he needs to meet with us? Give unto God what is rightfully His; ***tithe in prayer***.

Waiting in the Presence of God

Isaiah 40:31, But they that wait upon the LORD shall renew their strength; they shall mount up with wings as eagles; they shall run, and not be weary, and they shall walk, and not faint (KJV). The Merriam-Webster dictionary defines *'wait'* as staying in a place of expectation. We must be watchful and in a position of expectancy.

One of the challenges is when two or more individuals are speaking simultaneously. Therefore, confusion can arise, and offenses can occur. Chapter One looked at *"communication,"* which is the imparting or exchanging information or news. **Prayer** is a **two-way conversation between man and God**. Notice, *"it is a two-way conversation between the man and God."* This shows that we should not be the only ones talking but allow God to speak.

How often have you been asked to pray and do all the talking? Think about it, at what point did God get a chance to speak with you? You must be in a place of expectancy. At times, you need to stay in that place or position and wait for God to speak.

It is essential to hear the voice of the Lord. Sometimes, he may speak audibly. At other times the Holy Spirit speaks to us. *Psalms 29:3-5, "The voice of the Lord is over the waters; the God of glory thunders, the Lord thunders over the mighty. The voice of the Lord is powerful; the voice of the Lord is majestic. The voice of the Lord breaks the cedars..." (NIV).* God wants that particular time with you too. He has so much to share with you!

The dimensions of God become a reality when you can download from him. Allow God to download his messages through you so that you can walk in his will. Remember to give God a chance to talk to you (*See Chapter 8*). Ask God to provide you with active listening, understanding, and wisdom. Wait in His presence!

Study Question(s): What types of fasting do you think Jesus did throughout his ministry? Do you have an active fasting and prayer life?

_____

_____

_____

_____

_____

_____

_____

_____

_____

_____

_____

_____

_____

CHAPTER EIGHT

Are Prayer Points Effective?

> *Hebrews 4:12, For the word of God is alive and active. Sharper than any double-edged sword, it penetrates even to dividing soul and spirit, joints and marrow; it judges the thoughts and attitudes of the heart. NIV*

What are Prayer Points?

There are different ways that we can express ourselves in *prayer* before God. We can express through songs, by writing a letter to God, by finding scriptures that address the situation we are facing, or by *praying in tongues*.

Prayer points are also another way to make our requests known to God in a step-by-step process. It allows us to say or write specific things we want to focus on during our time with God. *Philippians 4:6, "Do not be anxious about anything, but in every situation, by prayer and petition, present your requests to God" (KJV)*.

Many believers or Children of God find praying challenging because they cannot find the words to say. Prayer points can help guide such individuals into conversations with God that provides structure and a sense of purpose. It is imperative to note that your relationship with God in *prayer* is unique, and no one can change that.

Writing down our thoughts can be very effective. The Psalmist, David, expressed himself in songs and *prayer points*. When you look at how David formulated his words and approach to God, it is clear that he had a strong relationship with Yahweh, regardless of the many mistakes. David took *prayer* to another level as he worshipped God, danced before him, and showed how much he loved him. Additionally, he used *prayer points* to speak out against the enemy and remind God that he trusted his promises.

The Word of God is a Weapon

Hebrews 4:12, "For the word of God is alive and powerful. It is sharper than the sharpest two-edged sword, cutting between soul and spirit, joint and marrow. It exposes our innermost thoughts and desires" (NLT). The scripture reminds us that God's word is like no other. His word has remained steadfast and stood the test of time.

The **Word of God** is likened to a *"two-edged"* sword. The Merriam-Webster dictionary defines a *two-edged sword* as having two cutting edges; in its nature, it is double-edged to perform good or evil acts. When we pray, the ***Word of God*** should always be our weapon of defense. Jesus Christ was the Living Word. He manifested the word throughout his teachings and used it to demonstrate the power of God.

The ***Word of God*** is given to man to become like a sharpshooter. It is one of the Armors of God. It allows us to rely on Scriptural authority rather than focusing on self. We must always be on guard and have this weapon (***Word of God***) ready for spiritual warfare, victory chants, healing and deliverance, and overcoming adversities. When we read the ***Word of God*** daily, it feeds the spirit-man in us. We can command and subdue the enemy and the kingdom of darkness through the power of the Holy Spirit.

The scriptures are evidence of things that have already happened or are to come. Many challenges faced today have already been experienced by men and women of ancient times. Daniel prayed the word thrice daily to build a relationship and remind God of his promises. Apostle Paul wrote to the churches in Corinth using the ***Word of God*** as the foundation to make things right.

Aligning the Word of God in Prayer

Like many in the Old and New Testaments, the Christian believer must know how to *align* with the Word of God. We **must** go deep into the word by looking for specific scriptures and examples that can handle the situations. We can write down our *prayer points* and find the scriptures that speak or declares the word according to the circumstance.

Using the scriptures and expressing the *prayer points* can help ignite the fire within us. Additionally, *prayer points* help some people to pray more effectively and purposefully to strengthen their relationship with God.

It is a matter of choice and not the only way to pray. Explore and discover what can help you have a meaningful prayer life and draw you closer to God.

Study Question(s): Have you used Prayer Points before? Do you base your Prayer Points on scriptural evidence?

_____

_____

_____

_____

_____

_____

_____

_____

_____

_____

_____

_____

_____

PART IV
LET US PRAY

CHAPTER NINE

Prophetic Intercessory Prayer

Romans 8:26, In the same way, the Spirit helps us in our weakness. We do not know what we ought to pray for, but the Spirit himself intercedes for us through wordless groans. NIV

What is intercession?

Intercession is a prayer or petition to God on behalf of someone. When you intercede, you ask Jesus to mediate on your behalf before God and help solve a problem. God sent His only begotten Son so that man could access grace and mercy. Jesus spent his time praying, interceding on behalf of a sinful generation.

Five traits used to identify an *intercessor* are courage, steadfastness, perseverance, consecration, and selflessness. Jesus possessed all these qualities and more. This allowed him to give his life and complete the will of His Father. He felt a *"burden"* that was like no other to redeem man from the law's curse.

Prayer and Intercessory Prayer

Apostle Paul always encouraged the church to **"pray without ceasing"** and to **"make supplications"** (requests known) unto God. In Corinthians, Paul admonished the saints to pray and reminded them, *"I am praying for you."* His life was spent preaching, teaching, and praying.

Prayer and *Intercessory Prayer* both address God. However, we should not only pray to God but learn how to pray with God (*Prophetic Intercessory Prayer*). We often focus on what we want God to do and not pray for God's will. In **Prophetic Intercessory Prayer**, we always pray with God in the Spirit. Jesus prayed for the will of his Father...Thy kingdom comes; thy will be done.

The intercessor doesn't select random scriptures. Instead, scriptures are chosen by the Holy Spirit. As *intercessory prayer* occurs, the intercessor connects with God, which causes a synchronized beating of God's heart and pulsations through the individual's body.

Subduing the Flesh

Jesus and Apostle Paul recognized the importance of gaining redemption for the sinners and the church. In the Garden of Gethsemane, Jesus agonized over his upcoming death. *Matthew 26:38-39, Then He said to them, "My soul is consumed with sorrow to the point of death. Stay here and keep watch with Me." 39 Going a little farther, He fell facedown and prayed, "My Father, if it is possible, let this cup pass from Me. Yet not as I will, but as You will" (NIV).*

At this point, Jesus was experiencing the limitations of the flesh based on the emotions within his mind. *"Let this cup pass from me"* showed that the flesh was weak, and Jesus would have to take the authority to subdue his fleshly desires.

Apostle Paul loved interceding for the church. He had a *"burden"* for the work of God. The people were failing and giving up. The church had become lukewarm. Paul knew that if the saints continued to pray without ceasing, God would bring them into His glorious power.

His prayer life was full of worship and songs. Paul prayed for wisdom and understanding. Most importantly, he prayed that God would give the body of Christ patience and strength to endure (*longsuffering*).

The Journey into Prayer

Prayer is the only way to interact with the Spirit. It also reveals your weaknesses. However, your weakness can become your strength. On the Day of Pentecost, the disciples gathered in the Upper Room to await the arrival of the Holy Spirit. Each of them had their struggles and demons to deal with. None of them was perfect. Yet still, they believed and gathered in expectancy to receive God's promise of the Comforter (*Holy Spirit*).

The disciples needed to be on one accord (unity). God had to remove unforgiveness, pride, and anything contrary to His will for their lives. He was uniquely aligning each individual and then transforming their minds and bringing them to a place of unity in the spirit to receive the tongues of Heaven. The men '*gave*' themselves into **prayer**, asking God to free them from the slavery of their minds. As men afflicted their souls, they provoked a reaction from God.

Building Capacity in God

The Oxford Learner's Dictionaries defines "***capacity***" as the number of things or people a container or space can hold. To gain capacity, we must have a hunger for the things of God. We must have a strong appetite for the **Word of God** and **prayer.** Without longing (desires), we cannot contain God.

In Daniel 5, King Belteshazzar received a written message

on the wall from God. The Prophet of God, Daniel, interpreted the statement by saying God had numbered the king's days. He had been *"weighed in the spirit"* (**tekel**) and did not measure up. Although he had not been **weighed** on a physical scale, his actions towards God had been counted. He lacked capacity, and his actions went against God's will. He could not host God because of idol worship and his disobedience in doing God's will. He was weightless. His life was worth nothing. Therefore, God spewed him out.

Prayer is more about what you become rather than what you have. Many Christians or believers are more about asking God for things. *Prayer* should be about how you wish to operate in God's kingdom, not just what you want from him. We may receive a *"yes"* or *"no"* from God, yet we **must** continue the journey. *Prayer* was designed to make you and bring out the best of God's work in you.

Moses stayed for forty days and forty nights when he went to the mountains. He went to meet with God to intercede for Israel. Moses encountered God through the burning bush after *"cooking in prayer"* and *"fasting"* for forty days. Yahweh promised Moses that he would become like a God before Pharaoh at this encounter. Moses had tapped into a dimension that transitioned him to a new level. He could see into time and things that would happen for generations. After returning from the mountains, he was full of fire for God's work. *Exodus 24:9, "When Moses came down from Mount Sinai with the two tablets of the Testimony in his hand, he did not know that the skin of his face was shining [with a unique radiance] because he had been speaking with God"* (AMP). He had built **capacity** in God.

When you have the **capacity**, you can function like God's character. You become what you "**host.**" Like Moses, you will become like a God before your enemies. You will operate like Yahweh himself!

Spiritual Network

Prayer is a migration in the spirit. It is the breath that the soul lives on. It takes us into **intimacy with God**. Without intimacy, we have no connection. Our power source is drained. Such **intimacy with God** sets us up for the impossible. It is how we take dominion over the Earth; the things God has promised us.

Within the Realm of the Spirit, there is a **spiritual network**. The host of this network is God. He is the source of power. Without the source of power, the servers cannot operate. Like an operating system that controls or manages a distinct set of computers (that work like one computer), God uses a spiritual operating system that owns or operates everything in the universe. He uses a mainframe system to complete multiple tasks within the universe. The Holy Spirit is the *"password."* You need this password to gain access to God.

A Computer's random-access memory (RAM) is crucial because it determines its performance. The RAM is the place where applications can store and access short-term data. Your mind is the RAM in your body. If your mind is unstable, corrupt, or confused, you will not be able to have a practical prayer life. Applications such as unforgiveness, hatred, and witchcraft will cause our minds to run out of storage. These sinful acts cause the Demonic Realm to have total control over the mind. When the mindset is corrupted, our prayer life becomes *obsolete*.

God's *spiritual network* allows a man to dominate the Earthly Realm. However, a man struggles to command things because of unbelief and sin. We cannot tap into the realms of power because we have not journeyed in the Spirit. The twenty-four Elders, Spirits, and the Angels of God operate in their assigned roles just as evil spirits, demons, and fallen angels operate in their roles. We must find our rightful place in God to join his network. We need the Holy Spirit to guide us daily. Then we can build capacity with God, hear his voice, and download his messages and assigned tasks for our life.

Study Question(s): How can I gain full access to God's Kingdom? What steps can I take to become a "commander" in the Earthly Realm?

_____

_____

_____

_____

_____

_____

_____

_____

_____

_____

_____

_____

_____

_____

CHAPTER TEN

Cook Yourself in Prayer

Leviticus 6:13, Keep the fire burning on the Altar continuously. It must not go out. MSG

Give Yourself to Prayer

The Greek word for *"give"* is **didomi**. It means *to cause, profuse, and give forth from oneself.* You step outside the norm when you *'give'* yourself into prayer. You ignite flames upon the enemy, subduing the flesh and going higher in the spirit. The Spirit-man is being filled with the Power of God. *Romans 8:11, "And if the Spirit of the One who raised Yeshua from the dead is living in you, then the One who raised the Messiah Yeshua from the dead will also give life to your mortal bodies through his Spirit living in you" (CJB).* Just imagine, you are like a ship carrying explosives that can go off any time!

We have been called to disarm Satan and his agents. Yet many Christians are living in fear. What is FEAR? **FEAR** is *False Evidence Appearing Real!* God did not give us the spirit of fear. He asks us to trust him. *Proverbs 3:5-6, "Trust in the*

LORD *with all your heart, And lean not on your understanding; In all your ways acknowledge Him, And He shall direct your paths"* (NKJV).

When Jesus entered any village, town, or city, he always came from the mountain top. *Why?* He knew that there were territorial spirits, and he had to take authority over every satanic agent and their plans before he entered. On Mount Olive, Jesus prayed to God, asking Him for strength to endure and complete his mission on Earth. He knew the path was challenging, and he continued to pray (*stirring the pot daily*) and kept the flames burning.

The Secret Place

There is a **secret place** in God that we can abide in. It is in the **secret place** that we find strength. The Psalmist David talks about an isolated place in *Psalms 27:5, "For in the day of trouble He will hide me in His shelter; In the secret place of His tent, He will hide me; He will lift me on a rock"* (AMP).

In *Psalms 91:1*, David declares that if we dwell under the shadow of the Almighty God (*secret place*), He will be our refuge and strength. Within you, the Spirit of God is that part of you that you can always rely upon. That means you seek Him and draw near to him. There are times when you need to withdraw to that *secret place* in you.

The Bible tells us in Exodus 33:7-8, *Moses took his tent and pitched it outside the camp, far from the camp, and called it the tabernacle of meeting. And it came to pass that everyone who sought the Lord went out to the tabernacle of meeting which was outside the camp. So it was, whenever Moses went out to the tabernacle, that all the people rose, and each man stood at his tent door and watched Moses until he had gone into the tabernacle (NKJV).* Moses understood what it meant to meet God in a place where there were no distractions and having an area to remain sacred to God at all times.

The *secret place* is where you find safety. God loves when we come to Him in prayer.

1. We must always have a **heart of worship** before we begin to pray.

2. **Acknowledge** Yahweh for His goodness and greatness to humanity.

3. We must **locate the names of God** for the situation at hand. Just like in a letter, you must first give your salutation. For example, Jehovah Jireh, my provider. There is none like him, and there will not be anyone like him.

There is a time and place for everything. Your prayer life may look different based on your circumstances and daily routines. However, there are times that you need that private moment with God, just as how he needs that time alone with you. Yes, God wants personal time with you too. Jesus said to his disciples, *"But when you pray, go away by yourself, shut the door behind you, and pray to your Father in private. Then your Father, who sees everything, will reward you"* *Matthew 6:6 (NLT)*.

Cooking Yourself in Prayer

The word *"cook"* means to subject (*something*) to the action of heat or fire during preparation. Most foods are prepared using heat. Before something is cooked, all ingredients are gathered and prepared to make a sumptuous meal.

Prayer has certain ingredients needed to take us into the place of intimacy with God.

1. We must **believe** that God can do exceedingly and above all we ask for.
2. We must **address** Him and acknowledge His presence.
3. We should have the heart to **love** others because God is love.

4. We must pray for the **will of God** at all times.

5. We should expect the **impossible** and never place limits on God.

You will likely look in the pot and *"stir"* the food Prayer is just like "cooking" food. We prepare with worship and enter His presence with thanksgiving in our hearts. Prophetic Worship brings us into a place to meet with God. As we worship, the fragrance of our worship must reach the Heavens. God wants to fill us with His Spirit. *1 Corinthians 15:45, So it is written: "The first man Adam became a living being; the last Adam, a life-giving spirit" (NIV).*

The ***Word of God*** is love and power in our hearts. We **must** let the kingdom of darkness know that every organ and part of our body is a willing participant in this migration process in the Spirit. As you read the ***Word of God*** and proclaim it as a weapon of warfare, the enemy knows that you are standing on God's promises. At this point, you **must** understand that God is not man. Therefore, He cannot lie. However, He can change His mind. He can do the impossible.

Our God is one of order and has specific protocols in place. We must address God through worship. Magnify and exalt the King of Kings and the Lord of Lords!

We must come to a place where self-conceit, pride, and self-doubt are no longer a part of our lives. When you touch that *Realm of Prayer*, your life can never be the same. God will shake the Heavens and the Earth on your behalf. Even the enemy becomes shocked at your blessings. Are you ready to provoke a reaction from God through your prayer?

Study Question(s): How often have I doubted God? Do I believe that God can do the impossible?

_____

_____

_____

_____

_____

_____

_____

_____

_____

_____

_____

_____

_____

_____

CONCLUSION

Prayer resets us spiritually, just like exercise physically resets our mind and body. Our spirit-man must be fed daily with God's word to gain strength to face the challenges in this life. The spirit-man is that part of us that intercedes and communicates the intentions of our hearts. Having the right mindset as we pray allows us to get God to respond. Sometimes we are limited by time to get to that ***secret place*** or the closet space. However, our hearts must always be in communication with God. The ***heart*** must always be praying.

To become the torch that burns, our prayer life must be consistent, setting aside time to meditate, going deeper in the word, and going higher in the spirit. Man's perception of ***prayer*** is not the same as God's perception. We should see through God's eyes and become selfless before him. Total surrender is needed, submission to God's will, and praying for the ***Will of God***.

We must eat the word, walk in the word, and pray the word.

If you don't pray, you will become the prey! We need appetite! Ask yourself: *How much of God can I contain? Do I have the required capacity? What is my weight in the Spirit?*

Prayer requires hunger and thirst after righteousness. We have all come short of his glory, but he rewards those that seek him diligently. Do not be like the Pharisees and Sadducees who only pray loudly for everyone to see. When you need that time with God, go to your personal space. Spend your time opening up yourself and allowing Jesus Christ to give you access to our Heavenly Father.

Sometimes, you may feel tired, oppressed, and weak. Remember, the word of God tells us in *Ecclesiastes 9:11*, *"I returned and saw under the sun, that the race is not to the swift, nor the battle to the strong, neither yet bread to the wise, nor yet riches to men of understanding, nor yet favor to men of skill; but time and chance happeneth to them all"* (*KJV*). Don't look at another man's prayer life and compare it to yours. Many will pass you on the track, but they will get tired. Some of them will even give up along the way. Remember, you must endure and journey in *prayer* through it all.

Many of you have been burdened for too long. Jabez was in a place where his life resembled pain. It was the inheritance he received when his mother gave him the name "Jabez" due to the pain and challenges in her life. *1 Chronicles 4:9-10: "Jabez was more honorable than his brothers. His mother had named him Jabez, saying, 'I gave birth to him in pain.' Jabez cried to the God of Israel, 'Oh that you would bless me and enlarge my territory! Let your hand be with me, and keep me from harm so that I will be free from pain.' And God granted his request."*

God wants to reset your prayer life. You have been searching for answers to your prayers for a while. God has given you some new tools to have a meaningful prayer life.

As you have gained new insights into what **prayer** is, **separating yourself**, and **entering the Spiritual Realm**, you now have the necessary tools to ignite the fire within you. Become a *'prayer and firebrand.'* Allow God to see himself in you. He is the fiery God, Esh Oklah, El Kanna: the Consuming Fire, Jealous God! Go forth now and *"Cook Yourself in Prayer! Come Out and Manifest!"* Selah

BONUS:

PROPHETIC PRAYER WATCHES

10 EFFECTIVE PRAYERS

PROPHETIC PRAYER WATCHES

Eight (8) Prayer Watches

The Greek word for *"watch"* is **parakoloutho´** which means to guard. The eight prayer watches are gates to enter the **Realm of Prayer**. The Child of God needs to stand at their post and pray effectively. *Habakkuk 2:1, "I will stand at my watch and station myself on the ramparts; I will look to see what he will say to me, and what answer I am to give to this complaint"* *(NIV)*. Before the doors can open, you must first go through the gates in the realm of prayer.

First Watch: The Evening Watch (6 pm to 9 pm)

Time of worship, meditation, brokenness, renewal, breaking strongholds – generational curses. This prayer watch is for serious believers who are determined to complete their mandate with God. Jesus, Peter, and Daniel prayed at this time based on their covenant with God.

Matthew 14:15-23, Lamentations 2:18-19, Exodus 27:21

Second Watch: The Midnight Watch (9 pm to 12 am)

Be watchful, meditate, time of breaking bondages, time of intercession, deliverance, declaring divine judgment on the enemy. During this watch, the enemy is given assignments and sabotage against God's people. It is a time to be strong and pray for protection for families, cities, and nations. At this period, all prophetic intercessors are called to go higher in the spirit to tear down and destroy the enemies' plans—a time to pray and subdue the flesh. Pray Psalms 59; 68:1-4

Psalms 63:6, Psalms 119:62, Acts 16:25

Third Watch: The Witching Hour (12 am to 3 am)

Demonic activity, witchcraft, destroying satanic altars, praying against satanic attacks, and praying for divine protection. This watch is full of spiritual activities and satanic attacks. It is the time of witchcraft activities. Do not be shaken by this. At this time, intercessors are called to go higher in the spirit as Satan summons warlocks, witches, sorcerers, and Satanists. When people are most vulnerable, as men are in a deep sleep, those that know how to intercede are needed at this time.

Luke 22:23, Mark 14:30, Psalms 91:5-6, 1 Kings 3:20

Fourth Watch: The Morning Watch (3 am to 6 am)

Time to command your day, activate your faith, time of decreeing miracles, coming against hindrances, breaking and nullifying the enemy's plans. During this watch, demons, evil spirits, and satanic agents go out to complete their assignments. It was during this hour that Israel was delivered from Egypt. This is the hour to command and decree God's will and speak God's word over your life.

Psalms 19:2, Exodus 12 and 14, Psalms 30:5, Job 38:12, Job 22:27-28, Lamentations 3:23

Fifth Watch: The Early Morning Watch (6 am to 9 am)

Preparation for the day, praying for healing in body, family, relationships, government, cities, and nations. This watch is the first watch of the day before the workday begins. Additionally, this was the Holy Spirit descended on the disciples in the Upper Room. It is the time to ask God to order your steps and entrust your workday to him, praying for renewed strength to complete daily tasks; and declaring healing in every area of your life.

Proverbs 16:3, Ephesians 4:12, Psalms 103:2-4

Sixth Watch: Time of Fulfillment (9 am to 12 pm)

Time to see God's word fulfilled in your life. Pray and ask him for forgiveness. During this time, Jesus was placed on the cross to be crucified (third hour). Reflect on God's love for us and his crucifixion's impact on our lives. We pray that God allows you to become selfless to complete His will in your life. Additionally, it is a time to pray for provision: ask God to provide the resources you need. This was when the Israelites went before God to ask him to provide what they needed to build his tabernacle. Take the opportunity to ask God to supply your needs so that you can bless His work too.

Romans 8:12-15, Matthew 27:45, Mark 15:25, Exodus 12:35-36, Philippians 4:13

Seventh Watch: Entering the Secret Place (12 pm to 3 pm)

Time of atonement, withdrawing to the Secret Place, praying for God to make himself known in the Nations through warning, signs, and wonders. During this time, Jesus atoned for the people's sins and did the Will of God the Father. It is also the time to ask God to keep you and your family safe from all satanic arrows and help you "dwell under the shadow of the Almighty." This watch is also the time when the sun shines brightest because it is midday. We pray not to become ensnared in the traps of the enemy or be led into temptations.

Psalms 91, Matthew 5:16, Proverbs 4:18, Acts 10:9

Eighth Watch: Renewed (3 pm to 6 pm)

During this watch, it is a time to reflect, meditate, and ask God to renew your mindset. It is also a time to remove idol worship, dismantling mental and physical strongholds, recurring cycles, idol worship, and old patterns. Additionally, it is a time to remind God of his defeating hell and the grave and taking the keys from the devil. Praying for deliverance, removing yourself from the kingdom of darkness, removing the veil, and receiving full access to God through his Son, Jesus Christ. Declaring that you "live in Christ" and "He Lives in You."

John 20, Galatians 2:20, Matthew 28:18-20, Ephesians 2:10

10 Effective Prayers

PRAYER TO WALK IN THE SPIRIT

"If we live by the Spirit, let us also walk by the Spirit" *(Galatians 5:25).*

Prayer Points:

1. My Father, My God, Holy Spirit, I was chosen before the foundation of the world to be holy and walk blameless before you. Please help me to walk in your perfect will like you commanded Abraham in Jesus' Mighty name (Gen. 17:1)

2. Oh My God, Keep me from justifying actions that grieve the Holy Spirit and from being trapped by the enemy (Eph. 4:30; Isa. 5:21).

3. God of Fire, let the Holy Spirit illuminate my mind (1 Thess.19). Bring conviction to those areas that are dull to me (Heb. 5:12-14). Keep me back from violating my conscience in Jesus' Name.

4. My Father, My God, help me not only to be a hearer of your Words but a doer of them (James 1:22)

5. God of Alignment, keep me in line with your Spirit to give me direction and guide me in the way of liberty, in the name of Jesus (Proverbs 3:5-6).

6. My Father, My God, ignite my heart and motivate me to move forward with the knowledge you give me in Jesus' Name (2 Timothy 3:7; 2 Peter 1:3-4).

7. My Father, My God, when the tests and challenges come at me from every side, help me to the inner part of me that I am strong in the spirit.

8. My Father, My God, clothe me with your Son, Jesus Christ so that I will not be weakened to satisfy my flesh and be able to walk into a place of no limits (Rom. 13:14).

9. My Father, My God, May the voice of the Spirit become my inner voice so that I will be aligned with you (Rom. 5:1).

10. My Father, My God, by the Power of the Holy Spirit at work in me, I barricade my life from every satanic opinion, and every prayer point will manifest over my life today in the name of Jesus.

DESIRING THE HOLY SPIRIT

John 4:24 - God [is] a Spirit: They who worship him must worship [him] in spirit and truth.

Prayer Points:

1. My Father, My God, Lord, I thank you for the gift of the Holy Spirit (1 John 4:13).

2. Spirit of the Living God, come upon me in Jesus' name and release me by fire now in Jesus' name (Act 1:8).

3. Oh God, My Father, Let the anointing of truth from the Spirit of God come upon my life (Heb. 3:7).

4. God of Direction and Clearance, let your Holy Spirit be my traffic guide day long in Jesus' name (Galatians 5:25)

5. Spirit of the Living God, lead me to more profound truths about the Kingdom (John 16:13).

6. My Father, My Maker, Spirit Divine, I make myself available for your tutelage and directions (Romans 8:14).

7. Oh God of Fire, purge whatever is in me that will resist the Holy Spirit by fire right now, in the name of Jesus.

8. My Father, My God, from today, the spirit of disobedience, shall not operate in my life in the name of Jesus (Romans 11:32).

9. Spirit of the Living God, fill me with hope, joy, and peace.

10. My Father, My God, by the power of the Holy Spirit, I barricade my life from every satanic opinion, and every prayer point will manifest over my life today in the name of Jesus.

DESTROYING FLESHLY DESIRES

John 16:13, However, when the Holy Spirit of truth comes, He will lead you [apostles] into all the truth. For He will not speak on His authority but will speak [only] what He hears [from the Father]. And He will tell you about the things that are to come.

Prayer Points:

1. My Father, the Ancient of Days, make me a portable altar to walk and operate in the Spirit of truth.

2. Oh Lord, the Everlasting Welder, make me firm in you and the Power of Your Greatness; put your whole armor upon me, that I may stand steadfast against the crafty assaults of the Devil (Eph. 6)

3. My Father, My God, eradicate me all fleshly desires that are contrary to the wishes of Your Spirit (Gal. 5:6).

4. God of Strength and Power, discipline me and bring every thought under submission to Your loving Lordship.

5. Oh God of Fire, like Moses' arms were held high during the battle for victory, lift my drooping heart

to reviving mode to journey into the realm of prayer (Eph. 6:18).

6. My Father, My God, I destroy the power of every satanic arrest in my life in the name of Jesus.

7. Oh my God, let satanic arresting agents; release me and die in the name of Jesus.

8. My Father, My God, remove from me the fleshly desires that are contrary to the wishes of Your Spirit (Gal. 5:6).

9. My Father, My God, I command every spiritual contamination in my spiritual life to receive cleansing by the blood of Jesus.

10. Oh God of Cleaning, let the Lord's brush scrub out every dirt in my spiritual pipe, in the name of Jesus.

11. Every dust-ridden and rusted spiritual pipe in my life, receive wholeness in the name of Jesus.

12. God of Fire, I command every power eating through my spiritual pipe to be roasted in the name of Jesus.

13. My God, I command every hole in my spiritual pipe to be closed in the name of Jesus.

14. Holy Spirit, open my eyes to see beyond the visible and make the invisible real to me, in the name of Jesus.

15. O Lord, let all strangers and wandering spirits flee from me and let the Holy Spirit take control in the name of Jesus.

16. The Freedom Fighting God, fight for me now and liberate my spirit to follow the leading of the Holy Spirit.

17. My Father, My God, by the power of the Holy Spirit in me, I barricade my life from every satanic opinion, and every prayer point will manifest in my life today in the name of Jesus.

RELEASE ME IN YOUR WILL

"Whatever you ask in my name, this I will do, that the Father may be glorified in the Son" (John 14:13).

If we align ourselves with God, we can have the confidence to ask for the things we desire because we know those things are also the things God desires. Therefore, we do not need to fear the things of this world or the weakness in ourselves.

By laying ourselves before God in prayer, we allow Him to change our hearts and work in the world around us. Fear is replaced by confidence for the believer who approaches God in prayer.

Prayer Points:

1. My Father, My God, in the name of my Lord Jesus Christ, I ask you to stir up within me the fullness of Your Holy Spirit.

2. Creator of Heaven and Earth, give me spiritual nutrients to grow in my relationship with you and use the gifts you have entrusted me with.

3. Oh God, My Father, help me remember that I do not know everything and that it is well because the Holy

Spirit understands everything. Fill me with the Holy Spirit and His understanding of everything in my life (John 14:26).

4. My Father, My Maker, help me to recognize You in the

   scriptures. Open my mind to understand Your truths, and use the word of God in faith even before I gain the proper understanding (John 14:17).

5. Master of the Eternal Garden, be the gardener of my life. Nourish the seeds of Heaven that You have already placed within me and make it grow so that Your love, ways, and the kingdom will always grow within me and produce much good fruit for others (Matt. 13:23).

6. God of Irrevocable Faith, deposit an unmovable trust in You, so I will always know that nothing is impossible even in my challenges (Luke 12:11-12).

7. My Father, My Creator, I say "yes" to whatever it is You are calling me to do

8. Oh God, My Father, I am your valuable currency. Spend me and keep the change.

9. My Father, My God, by the Power of the Holy Spirit at work in me, I barricade my life from every satanic

opinion, and every prayer point will manifest over my life today in the name of Jesus.

RELEASING MY FAMILY FROM BONDAGE

Acts 16:31, And they said, "Believe on the Lord Jesus Christ, and thou shalt be saved, and thy house."

Prayer Points:

1. My Father, My God, in the name of Jesus, I thank you for the salvation of my soul today.

2. Oh God, My Father, in the name of Jesus, I thank you for fighting and winning my battles on the cross of Calvary.

3. My Father, in the name of Jesus, I thank you for my family; you have already heard me.

4. God of Freedom, I release myself from every household bondage in my lineage in the name of Jesus.

5. Fire of the living God, like you, came down in the days of Elijah, consuming every chain of poverty, addiction, oppression, and limitation in my life today (1 Kings 18:38)

6. Holy ghost fire, like Elisha's days, sends down strange animals to consume every agent that has held down my finances and the finance of my family (2 Kings 2:23-24).

7. Heavenly Father, just like the angel rolled away from the stone from the tomb of Jesus, let my angel roll away every stone trapping the destiny of my family and me in a tomb (Matthew 28:2).

8. I release confusion and destruction into the camp of every kidnapper of my family's destiny today.

9. Heavenly Father, as the sea opened and swallowed the enemies of your people who held them in captivity for years. Let the sea swallow every ancestral spirit that has kept my family bound.

10. Let the mighty arm of God, which broke the chains of Paul and Silas in prison, break every chain connecting me to my past and restricting me from the future God has planned for my family and me.

11. Lion of the Tribe of Judah, just as you delivered Daniel and the three Hebrew children from the hands of their oppressors, deliver my family and me from the bondage of poverty, penury, and failure (Daniel 6:1-28)

12. Ballistic missiles from the Heavenly places begin to bombard every coven where my family's glory is hidden in Jesus' Name.

13. Any doors of setting evil spirits loose that I have

14. opened in my family, over my children, I close them today in Jesus' name.

15. My Father, My God, by the Power of the Holy Spirit at work in me, I barricade my life from every satanic opinion, and every prayer point will manifest over my life today in the name of Jesus.

MY CHILDREN'S DESTINY IS SECURED

Psalm 91:10: There shall no evil befall thee, neither shall any plague come nigh thy dwelling.

Proverbs 22:6 (ESV): Train up a child in the way he should go; even when he is old, he will not depart from it.

Psalm 127:3 (ESV): Behold, children are a heritage from the LORD, the fruit of the womb a reward.

Prayer Points:

1. My Father, My God, I thank you for children are your

   heritage and the fruit of the womb a reward (Psalm 127:3)

2. Oh God, help me train my children how they should go; even when he is old, he will not depart from it (Prov. 22:6).

3. My Father, My God, orders all my children's steps in the right direction. Let the Angels of the Lord always protect my children from danger in Jesus' name.

   Oh God of Wisdom, inflict my children with your wisdom for your great purpose in Jesus' name.

4. My God, My Savior, lead not my children into

Temptation, but deliver them from all evil in Jesus' name.

5. Oh God of Mercy, Today I separate my children from every ungodly influence in Jesus' name. Let mercy prevail over judgment in my children's life from this hour, this day, in the name of Jesus.

6. My Father, My God, help me teach them diligently, talk with them respectfully, and give instructions that please you in Jesus' name (Prov. 1:8-9).

7. The Stirred-Up God, let there be confusion between my children and any satanic influence in their life in Jesus' name.

8. My Father, My God, Father, if my child is a satanic influence to other children, separate him from those innocent children and deliver him today in Jesus' name.

9. Oh God of Undisputable Love, help me not spare the rod, but to love them diligently and discipline them to walk according to Your will (Prov. 13:24).

10. God that set Daniel free, deliver my children from idolatry, perversion, adultery, stealing, lying, smoking, drug addiction, pornography, and any evil devil work in Jesus' Mighty Name.

11. Every satanic agent, release my children from all strongholds and die by fire now in Jesus' name.

12. My Father, prosper my children and cause them to fulfill destiny and purpose in you in Jesus' name.

13. My Father, My God, by the Power of the Holy Spirit at work in me, I barricade my life from every satanic opinion, and every prayer point will manifest over my life today in the name of Jesus.

SECURING MY MARRIAGE

Hebrews 13:4-5, Marriage is honorable among all, and the bed undefiled; but fornicators and adulterers God will judge. Let your conduct be without covetousness; be content with such things as you have. He has said, "I will never leave you nor forsake you."

Mark 10:9, What God hath joined together let no man put asunder.

Prayer Points:

1. My Father, My God, Father, any human or spirit beings working to put my marriage asunder shall not succeed in Jesus' name (Mark 10:9)

2. Oh God, Your Word says that my husband is to be the head of our home. Give him a heart that desires to seek You and be led by Your Word as he leads our family in Jesus' name (Eph. 5:23).

3. My Father, My God, Father Lord, let all giants standing against peace and unity in my marriage be pulled down now in the name of Jesus (Luke 10:19).

4. Oh God of Wisdom, help me not be swayed by society norms but seek to follow Your Word, be the wife my husband needs, and submit as you have

commanded (Eph. 5:22-24).

5. My God, My Savior, let all powers encamping against my home and entire family line become confused and scattered in the name of Jesus (Isa. 54:15).

6. Oh God of Fire, let every power of the oppressors in my marriage revolt against each other in the name of Jesus (Zachariah 9:8).

7. My Father, My God, give each of us a heart that longs to seek You first. Help us realize that a relationship with You is the foundation of a successful marriage (Matt. 6:33).

8. Oh God of Fire, Lord Jesus, let your power work mightily in every difficult situation in my marriage in the name of Jesus (Jer. 32:27).

9. My Father, My God, I bind you the strongman working against me in the heart of my husband/wife and all his/her relatives in the name of Jesus (Matt. 12:29).

10. Oh my God, I render the power of the strongman working in my family utterly impotent from today in the name of Jesus.

11. My Father, My Maker, I receive victory over the host

12. of wickedness surrounding my marriage in the name of Jesus (Prov. 11:21).

13. Let all the trouble-makers of my marriage be disbanded and be confused in the name of Jesus (Gal 5:10).

14. Oh God of Thunder, every satanic storm in my marriage be silenced in the name of Jesus (Psalms 107:29).

15. God of Abraham, God of Elijah, God of my Prophets, answer all powers asking, "Where is my God?"

16. Let the blood of Jesus cleanse every evil label and evil pattern in my family lineage in the name of Jesus (Rev. 12:11).

17. I prophesy the life of Christ to every dead blessing in my marriage, my life, and the life of my partner in the name of Jesus.

18. I speak life into my marriage, let the life-giving spirit of Christ quicken my home unto joy, peace, unity, and prosperity in Jesus' mighty name.

19. My Father, My God, by the Power of the Holy Spirit at work in me, I barricade my life from every satanic opinion, and every prayer point will manifest over my life today in the name of Jesus.

DELIVERANCE FROM FINANCIAL OPPRESSION

1 John 3:8, He that committeth sin is of the devil; for the devil sinneth from the beginning. For this purpose, the Son of God was manifested so that he might destroy the works of the devil.

Prayer Points:

1. d, I reject every form of demonic oppression in Jesus' name.

2. Every spiritual anchor of financial failure attached to my life receive the ax of fire in the name of Jesus.

   Oh Lord, cleanse my hands from failure and financial collapse in Jesus' name.

3. Every strange money in my possession, be flushed out by the blood of Jesus.

4. My name, business, and handiwork will not record anything for the spirit of financial collapse in Jesus' name.

5. Oh Lord, rescue my finances from every satanic well, in Jesus' name.

6. Oh Lord, let all the powers oppressing my finances sit on the seat they constructed for me, in the name of Jesus.

7. Oh Lord, let all the powers oppressing my finances sit on the seat they constructed for me, in the name of Jesus.

8. Every tree of heaviness, procrastination, and discouragement operating in any area of my life, be cut down by the ax of fire, in Jesus' name.
   Oh Lord, give me the key to any good things you have kept in Your bank for me, in the name of Jesus.

9. Every stronghold of loss is dashed to pieces in the name of Jesus.

10. Every stronghold of debt, fashioned against my finances, be dashed to pieces in the name of Jesus.

11. Every satanic traffic warden, directing profit away from my career, business, and handiwork, receive the hailstones of fire in Jesus' name.

12. Whatever the enemies say would be impossible with my hands, your hands, hear the word of the Lord, begin to perform the impossible, in the name of Jesus.

13. Anointing to prosper, fall upon my hands, in the name of Jesus.

14. I release my hands from every satanic bondage affecting my finances in the name of Jesus.

15. You spirit of confusion and satanic inspiration of overdraft, loose your hold upon my life and business in the name of Jesus.

16. Every anchor of financial collapse affecting my finances, be uprooted by the ax of fire, in the name of Jesus.

17. By the fire arrows, I challenge all the agencies of financial collapse, fashioned against my finances, in the name of Jesus.

18. Every demon, strongman, and associated spirit of financial collapse receive the hailstones of fire and be roasted beyond remedy, in Jesus' name.

19. Oh Lord, prosper me beyond my wildest imaginations, and make me a candidate of the Abrahamic blessings in Jesus' name.

20. My Father, My God, by the Power of the Holy Spirit at work in me, I barricade my life from every satanic opinion, and every prayer point will manifest over my life today in the name of Jesus.

DELIVERANCE FROM DREAM CRIMINALS

Genesis 37:19-20 Here comes the dreamer!" they said. "Come on, let's kill him and throw him into one of these cisterns. We can tell our father, 'A wild animal has eaten him.' Then we'll see what becomes of his dreams!"

Prayer Points:

1. My Father, My God, I praise you today that at the name of Jesus every knee should bow, in Heaven and on earth and under the Earth, and every tongue confess that Jesus Christ is Lord (Phil. 2:10-11)

2. Oh God, arise and retrieve back my dream from the hands of my enemies, in the name of Jesus.

3. Anything or anyone blocking my memory from remembering some of my dreams, be frustrated, in the name of Jesus.

4. Every night and dream attack and its consequences should be nullified in Jesus' name.

5. I stand against every dream defeat and its effects in the name of Jesus.

6. Let all satanic designs of oppression against me in dreams and visions be frustrated in the name of Jesus.

7. I reverse any defeat that I have ever suffered in the dream in the name of Jesus.

8. Let every demonic influence targeted at destroying my vision, dreams, and ministry receive total disappointment in the name of Jesus.

9. Every cause of being harassed in the dream by a familiar face in my life be nullified by the blood of Jesus.

10. I paralyze all the night feeders and forbid their foods in my dream, in the name of Jesus.

11. All pursuers in my dream begin to pursue themselves in Jesus' name.

12. Any anti-progress material fired into my life through dreams, be nullified in the name of Jesus.

13. Every sickness planted in the dream into my life, get out now and go back to the sender, in the name of Jesus.

14. I crush every dream of poverty to the ground in the name of Jesus.

15. I paralyze the spirit that brings bad dreams to me in the name of Jesus.

16. Every anti-prosperity dream, die in the mighty name of Jesus.

17. Every power planting affliction into my life in my dreams be buried alive in the name of Jesus.

18. Every evil dream that other people have had about me, I cancel them in the astral world, in the name of Jesus.

19. I resist the threat of death in my dream, in the name of Jesus.

20. All powers that make me forget my dream, I am not your candidate, expire, expire, expire, in the name of Jesus.

21. By the power in the blood of Jesus, I cancel the maturity dates of any evil dreams in the name of Jesus.

22. My dreams, joys, and breakthroughs, buried in the dark world, are reversed now in Jesus' name.

23. By the power in the blood of Jesus, I command all dream and vision killers working against the manifestation of my good dreams and visions to be paralyzed.

24. Oh God of promotion, promote me beyond my wildest dreams, that they will be surprised in the name of Jesus when they come looking.

25. My Father, My God, by the Power of the Holy Spirit at work in me, I barricade my life from every satanic opinion, and every prayer point will manifest over my life today in the name of Jesus.

CANCELLING THE SPIRIT OF UNTIMELY DEATH

Psalms 118:17, I shall not die, but live, and declare the works of the Lord.

Prayer Points:

1. My Father, My God, In the name of Jesus, I declare that I shall not die but live to declare the works of God in the land of the living in Jesus' name. (Psalms 79:11).

2. By the hedge of Your protection, Oh Lord, preserve those appointed to die this year in my family, church, and this neighborhood in Jesus' name.

3. By the blood of Jesus, I wipe out my names from the register of premature death in Jesus' name.

4. Every arrow of slow death issued against my family and I backfire now in Jesus' name.

5. I will not sleep the sleep of death; I will not run the race of death and will not fall unto death in Jesus' name (Psalms 13:3, Act 20:9).

6. I declare my marriage will not lead me to the grave untimely, in Jesus' name.

7. My destiny that has been buried in the coffin or cemetery, by the power of the resurrection, I exhume

you, in the name of Jesus.

8. No weapon of death fashioned against me shall prosper, and any evil that revolts against me in judgment shall be condemned, in the name of Jesus (Isa. 54:17).

9. I reject every sickness unto death in the name of Jesus.

10. Any power planning to poison me, eat your poison and die in my place in the name of Jesus. And if I have eaten or drank poison in the past that is affecting my health, today be purged out by the blood of Jesus (Say I drink the blood of Jesus).

11. Terminal sickness programmed to kill me before my time, die by fire in the name of Jesus.

12. Every ancestral covenant of premature death made against my life on any evil altar, break by fire in the name of Jesus.

13. Every power jingling the bell of death on my destiny, you and your bell die by fire in the name of Jesus.

14. Spirit of premature death pursuing me from the grave of my ancestors, run back to your grave and settle yourself there, in the name of Jesus.

15. Garment of sudden death in my body, come out by the fire in the name of Jesus.

16. Eaters of flesh and drinkers of blood assigned against my life, receive the judgment of death and die in the name of Jesus.

17. Any power in my family assigned to cut short my life, die in my place, in Jesus' name.

18. Blood of Jesus, deliver my soul from the spirit of death in the name of Jesus.

19. Every power using the dream of my late relation to swallow my virtues, catch fire, in Jesus' name.

20. Any part of my body deposited in the graveyard, catch fire and roast to ashes, in Jesus' name.

21. My Father, My God, by the Power of the Holy Spirit at work in me, I barricade my life from every satanic opinion, and every prayer point will manifest over my life today in the name of Jesus.

22. My Father, My God, by the Power of the Holy Spirit at work in me, I barricade my life from every satanic opinion, and every prayer point will manifest over my life today in the name of Jesus.

Glossary

affliction: something that causes pain or suffering (p.24)

Amidah (Hebrew): "the standing prayer" consists of nineteen blessings (p.4)

communicate: to commune, to converse confidentially and sympathetically (p.5).

dialaleo⁻(Greek): to speak together, to talk with (p.5)

didomi (Greek): to cause, profuse, give forth from one's self (p.82)

demonize: to portray (someone or something) as evil or as worthy of contempt or blame (p.29)

glossolalia (Greek-German): the phenomenon of (apparently) speaking in an unknown language, especially in religious worship (p.48)

homilieo: to converse with, talk about: with one (p.5)

intercessory: the act of interceding; prayer, petition, or request in favor of another (p.74)

nesteia (Greek): abstinence (p.58)

nestuo (Greek): to abstain from food (p.59)

obsolete: no longer in use or no longer helpful (p.79)

Glossary cont'd...

perception: the ability to see, hear or become aware of something through the senses (p.19)

prayer: can be thought of as uttering or communicating words to our Heavenly Father that comes from our inner thoughts (p.3)

Selah: praise, pause (p.91)

Shema (Hebrew): "prayer of faith" is even more critical because it focuses on one's faith and knowing that there is only one God (p.4)

shod: means wearing shoes (p.41)

simultaneous: existing or occurring at the same time - exactly coincident (p.64)

ta'anit or ta'anis (Hebrew): abstains from all food and drink (p.59)

tefillah (Hebrew): prayer (p.4).

two-edged (double-edged): having two cutting edges (p.41)

Underworld: the place of departed souls (p.27)

Bible References:

Amplified Bible, Classic Edition (AMPC)

Berean Study Bible (BSB)

Contemporary English Version (CEV)

King James Version (KJV)

Messenger Bible (MSG)

New International Version (NIV)

New Living Translation (NLT)

New King James Version (NKJV)

Notes

Notes

Notes